DARIUSZ GRZYWACZ

CLASSIC FIGHTERS

colouring book

HAWKER HURRICANE

The Hawker Hurricane was a British single-seat fighter aircraft that was designed and predominantly built by Hawker Aircraft Ltd for the Royal Air Force (RAF). The aircraft became renowned during the Battle of Britain, accounting for 60% of the RAF's air victories in the battle, and served in all the major theatres of the Second World War.

GENERAL CHARACTERISTICS

Crew: 1
Length: 32 ft 3 in (9.84 m)
Wingspan: 40 ft 0 in (12.19 m)
Height: 13 ft 1½ in (4.0 m)
Wing area: 257.5 ft² (23.92 m²)
Empty weight: 5,745 lb (2,605 kg)
Loaded weight: 7,670 lb (3,480 kg)
Max. takeoff weight: 8,710 lb (3,950 kg)
Powerplant: 1 × Rolls-Royce Merlin XX liquid-cooled V-12, 1,185 hp (883 kW)

PERFORMANCE

Maximum speed: 340 mph (547 km/h)
Range: 600 mi (965 km)
Service ceiling: 36,000 ft (10,970 m)
Rate of climb: 2,780 ft/min (14.1 m/s)

ARMAMENT

Guns: 4 × 20 mm (.79 in) Hispano Mk II cannon
Bombs: 2 × 250 or 500 lb (110 or 230 kg) bombs

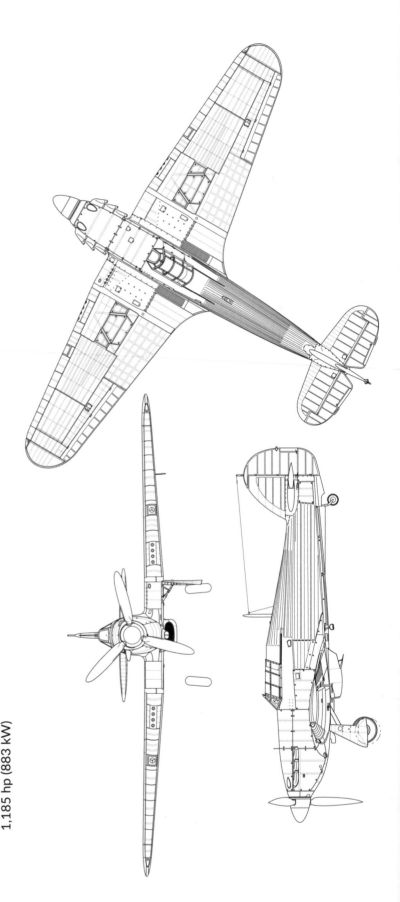

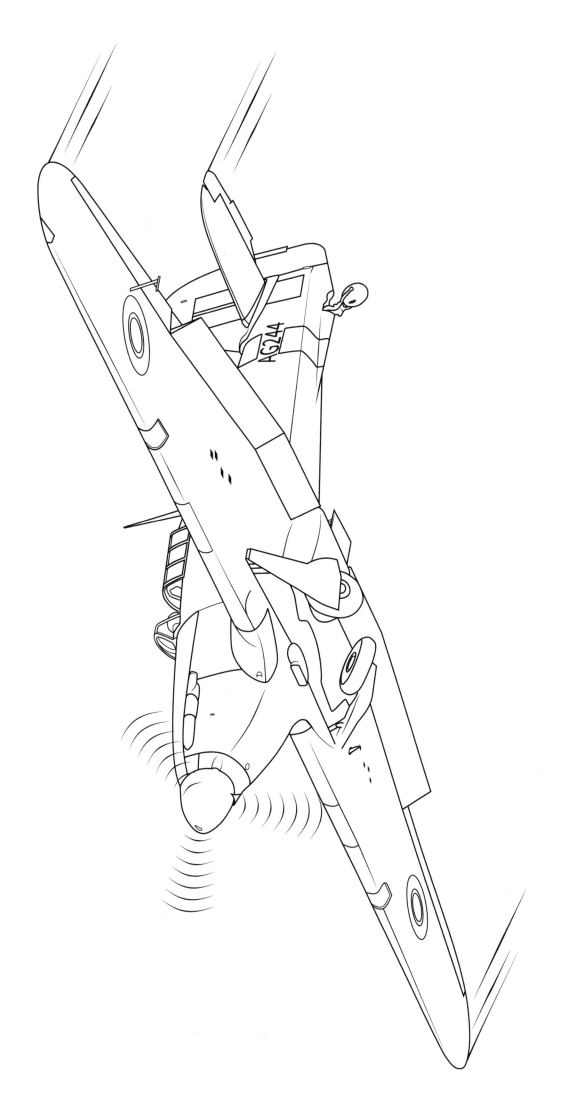

SUPERMARINE SPITFIRE

The Supermarine Spitfire was a British single-seat fighter aircraft that was used by the RAF and many other Allied countries before, during and after the Second World War. The Spitfire was built in many variants and was produced in greater numbers than any other British aircraft. It was also the only British fighter to be in continuous production throughout the war.

GENERAL CHARACTERISTICS

Crew:	1
Length:	29 ft 11 in (9.12 m)
Wingspan:	36 ft 10 in (11.23 m)
Height:	11 ft 5 in (3.86 m)
Wing area:	242.1 ft2 (22.48 m2)
Empty weight:	5,065 lb (2,297 kg)
Loaded weight:	6,622 lb (3,000 kg)
Max. takeoff weight:	6,700 lb (3,039 kg)
Powerplant:	1× Rolls-Royce Merlin 45[nb 15] supercharged V12 engine, 1,470 hp (1.096 kW)

PERFORMANCE

Maximum speed:	370 mph (595 km/h)
Combat radius:	410 nmi (470 mi (756 km))
Service ceiling:	36,500 ft (11,125 m)
Rate of climb:	2,600 ft/min (13.2 m/s)

ARMAMENT

Guns: 4 × 20mm Hispano Mk II cannon (120 rounds per gun)
        C wing (Alt.)
        2 × 20mm Hispano Mk II (120 rounds per gun)
        4 × 303 in Browning Mk II* machine guns (350 rounds per gun)

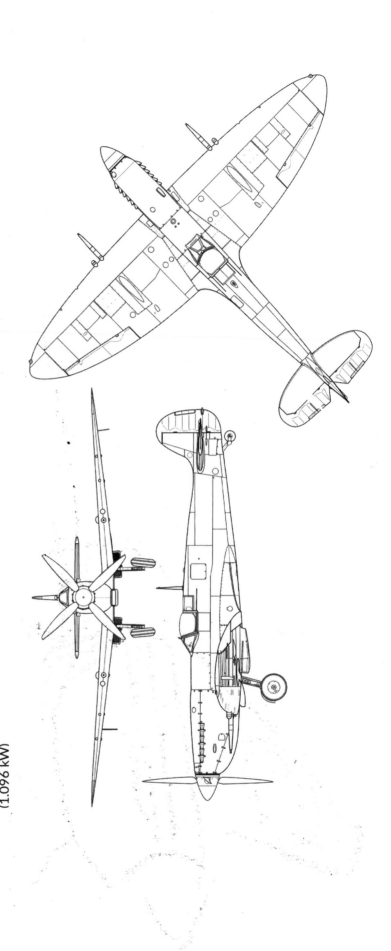

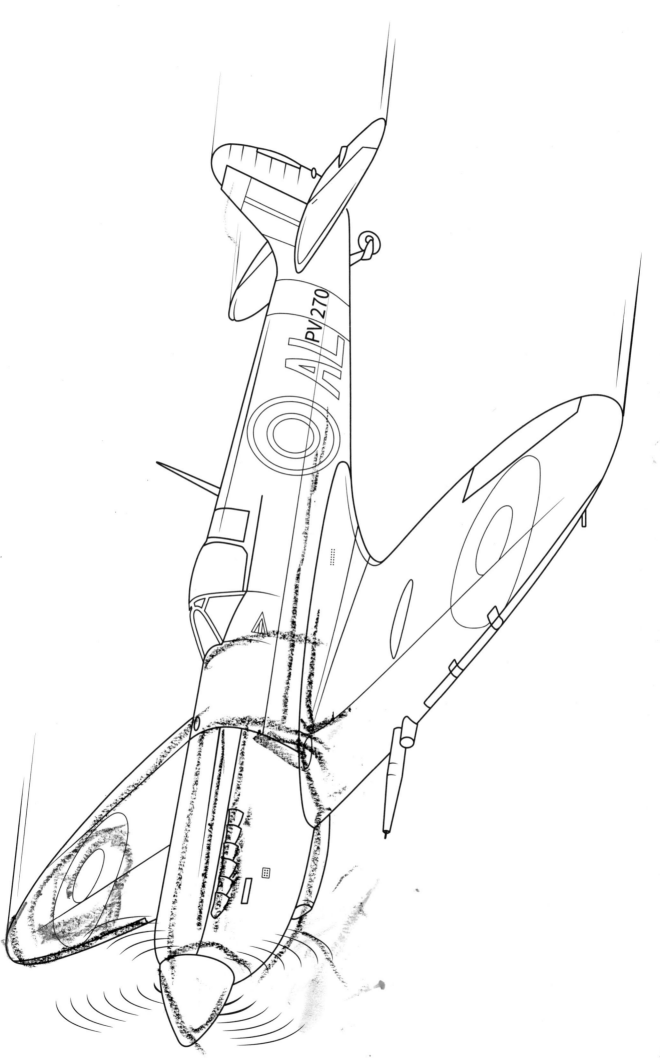

MESSERSCHMITT BF 109 G "GUSTAV"

The G series, or „Gustav", was introduced in mid-1942. The most widely produced model of the Messerschmitt Bf 109 fighter. Used in all theaters of war.

GENERAL CHARACTERISTICS

Crew:	1
Length:	8.95 m (29 ft 7 in)
Wingspan:	9.925 m (32 ft 6 in)
Height:	2.60 m (8 ft 2 in)
Wing area:	16.05 m² (173.3 ft²)
Empty weight:	2,247 kg (5,893 lb)
Loaded weight:	3,148 kg (6,940 lb)
Powerplant:	1 × Daimler-Benz DB 605A-1 liquid-cooled inverted V12, 1,475 PS

PERFORMANCE

Maximum speed:	640 km/h (398 mph) at 6,300 m (20,669 ft)
Cruise speed:	590 km/h (365 mph) at 6,000 m (19,680 ft)
Range:	850 km (528 mi) 1,000 km (621 mi) with droptank
Service ceiling:	12,000 m (39,370 ft)
Rate of climb:	17.0 m/s (3,345 ft/min)

ARMAMENT

Guns:	2 × 13 mm (.51 in) synchronized MG 131 machine guns with 300 rounds per gun 1 × 20 mm (.78 in) MG 151/20 cannon as centerline Motorkanone with 200 rpg.

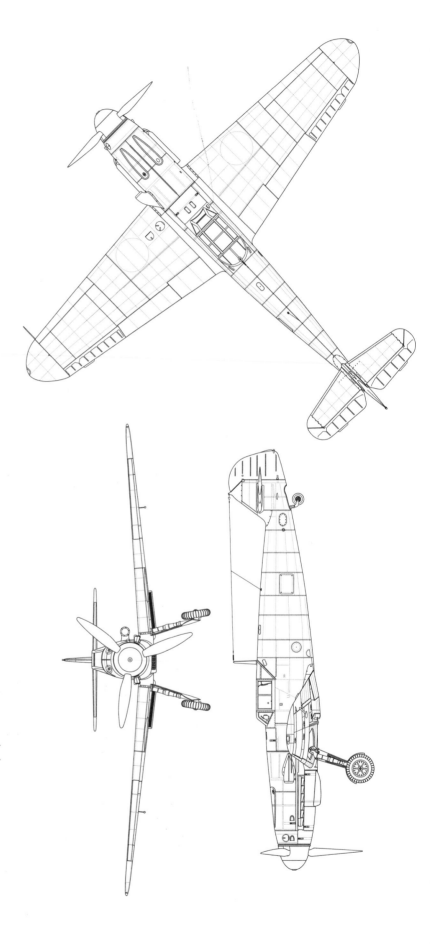

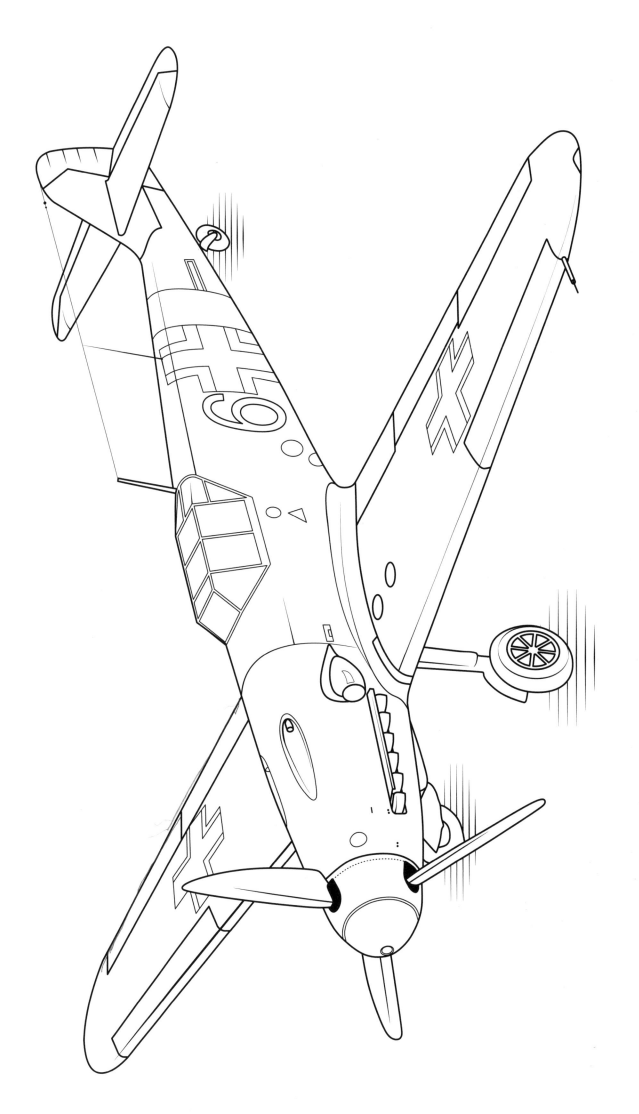

FOCKE-WULF FW 190 A

The Focke-WulfFw 190 Würger (English: Shrike) is a German single-seat, single-engine fighter aircraft designed by Kurt Tank in the late 1930s and widely used during World War II.
The twin-row BMW 801 radial engine that powered the Fw 190 to lift larger loads than the Bf 109, allowing its use as a day fighter, fighter-bomber, ground-attack aircraft and, to a lesser degree, night fighter.

GENERAL CHARACTERISTICS

Crew:	1
Length:	9.00 m (29 ft 5 in)
Wingspan:	10.51 m (34 ft 5 in)
Height:	3.95 m (12 ft 12 in)
Wing area:	18.30 m² (196.99 ft²)
Empty weight:	3,200 kg (7,060 lb)
Loaded weight:	4,417 kg (9,735 lb)
Powerplant:	1 × BMW 801 D-2 radial engine 1,250 kW (1,700 PS)

PERFORMANCE

Maximum speed:	656 km/h (408 mph) at 19,420 ft (5,920 m)
Range:	800 km (500 mi)
Service ceiling:	11,410 m (37,430 ft)
Rate of climb:	15 m/s (2,953 ft/min)

ARMAMENT

Guns:	2 × 13 mm (.51 in) synchronized MG 131 machine guns with 475 rpg
4 × 20 mm MG 151/20 E cannon with 250 rpg, synchronized in the wing roots and 140 rpg free-firing outboard in mid-wing mounts.

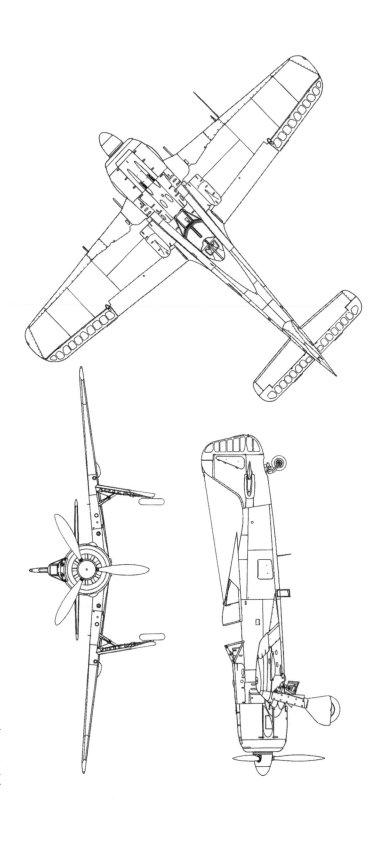

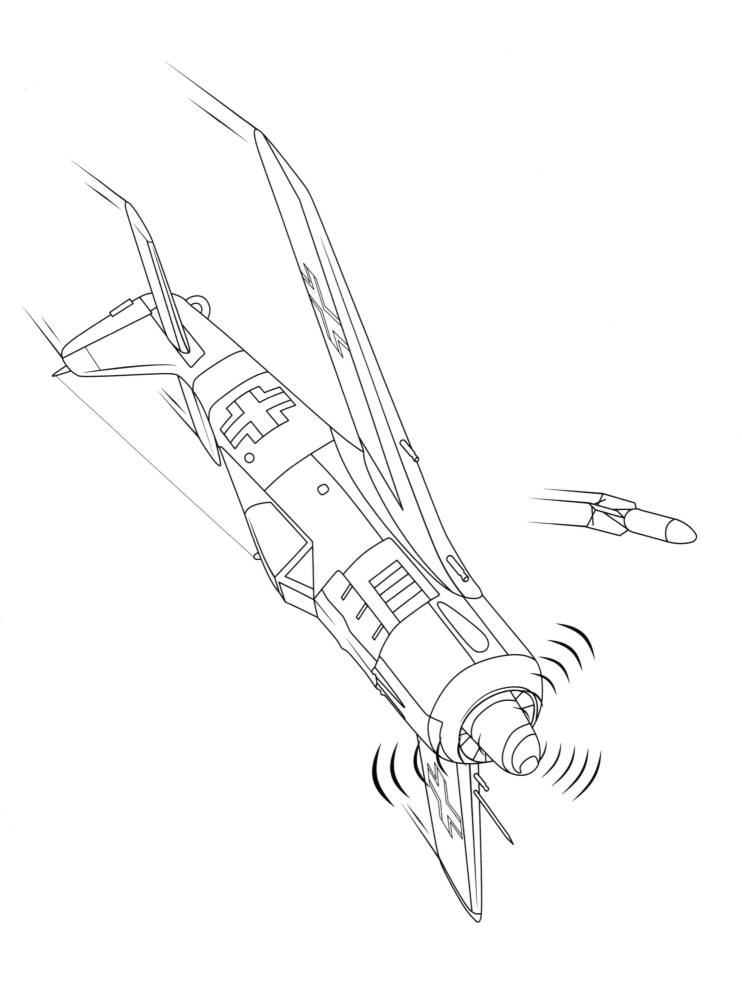

HAWKER TYPHOON

The Hawker Typhoon (Tiffy in RAF slang), was a British single-seat fighter-bomber, produced by Hawker Aircraft. It was intended to be a medium–high altitude interceptor. When the Luftwaffe brought the formidable Focke-Wulf Fw 190 into service in 1941, the Typhoon was the only RAF fighter capable of catching it at low altitudes.

GENERAL CHARACTERISTICS

Length:	31 ft 11.5 in (9.73 m)
Wingspan:	41 ft 7 in (12.67 m)
Height:	15 ft 4 in (4.66 m)
Wing area:	279 ft^2 (29.6 m^2)
Empty weight:	8,840 lb (4,010 kg)
Loaded weight:	11,400 lb (5,170 kg)
Max. takeoff weight:	13,250 lb (6,010 kg)
Powerplant:	[nb 23] 1 × Napier Sabre IIA, IIB or IIC liquid-cooled 2,180hp (1,626 kW)

PERFORMANCE

Maximum speed:	412 mph (663 km/h) [nb 25]
Range:	510 mi (821 km) [nb 25]
Service ceiling:	35,200 ft (10,729 m)
Rate of climb:	2,740 ft/min (13.59 m/s) [nb 26]

ARMAMENT

Guns:	4 × 20 mm Hispano Mk II cannon
Rockets:	8 × RP-3 unguided air-to-ground rockets.
Bombs:	2 × 500 lb (227 kg) or 2 × 1,000 lb (454 kg) bombs

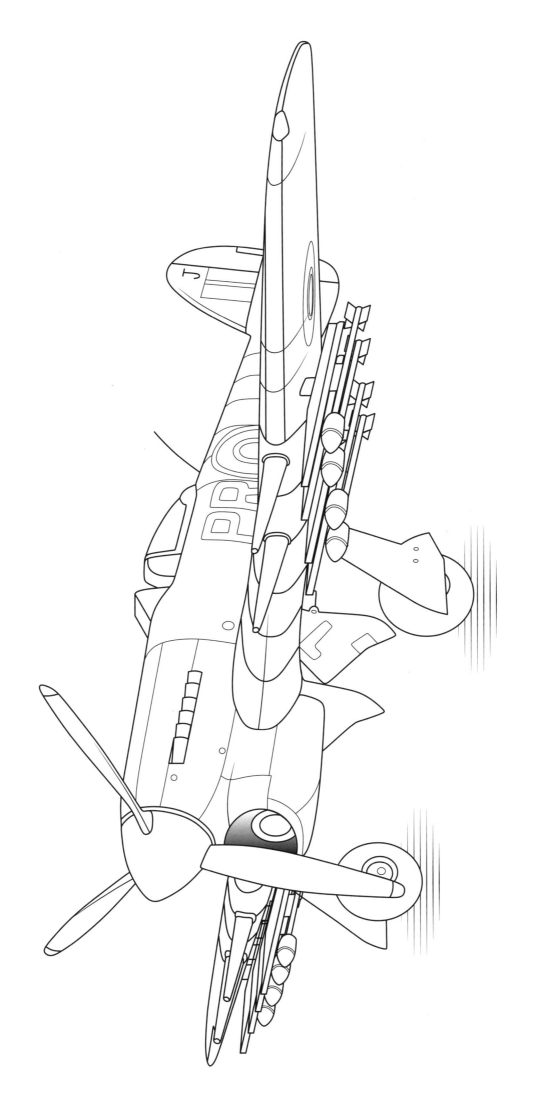

MIKOYAN-GUREVICH MIG-15

The Mikoyan-Gurevich MiG-15 was a jet fighter aircraft developed by Mikoyan-Gurevich OKB for the Soviet Union. The MiG-15 was one of the first successful jet fighters to incorporate swept wings to achieve high transonic speeds. In combat over Korea, it outclassed straight-winged jet day fighters which were largely relegated to ground attack roles.

GENERAL CHARACTERISTICS

Crew:	1 or 2
Length:	10.08 m (33 ft 1 in)
Wingspan:	10.08 m (33 ft 1 in)
Height:	3.7 m (12 ft 2 in)
Wing area:	20.6 m2 (222 sq ft)
Empty weight:	3,630 kg (8,003 lb)
Gross weight:	5,000 kg (11,023 lb)
Max takeoff weight:	6,105 kg (13,459 lb)
Powerplant:	1 × Klimov VK-1 centrifu gal flow turbojet, 26.5 kN (6,000 lbf) thrust

PERFORMANCE

Maximum speed:	1,059 km/h (658 mph; 572 kn) at sea level
Range:	1,240 km (771 mi; 670 nmi)
Service ceiling:	15,500 m (50,853 ft)
Rate of climb:	51.2 m/s (10,080 ft/min) at sea level

ARMAMENT

Guns: 2 x NR-23 23 mm (0.906 in) cannon in the lower left fuselage (80 rounds per gun, 160 rounds total)
1 x Nudelman N-37 37 mm (1.457 in) can non in the lower right fuselage (40 rounds total)
2 x 100 kg (220 lb) bombs, drop tanks, or unguided rockets on 2 underwing hardpoints.

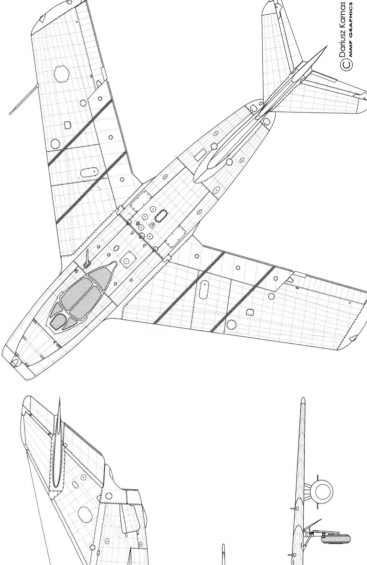

© Dariusz Karnas
MMP GRAPHICS

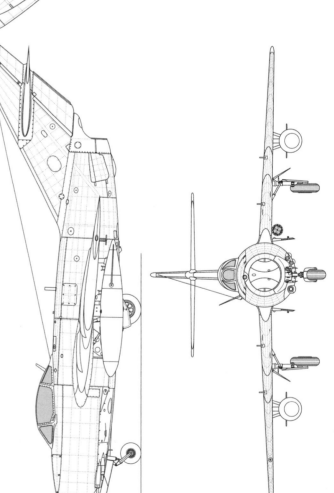

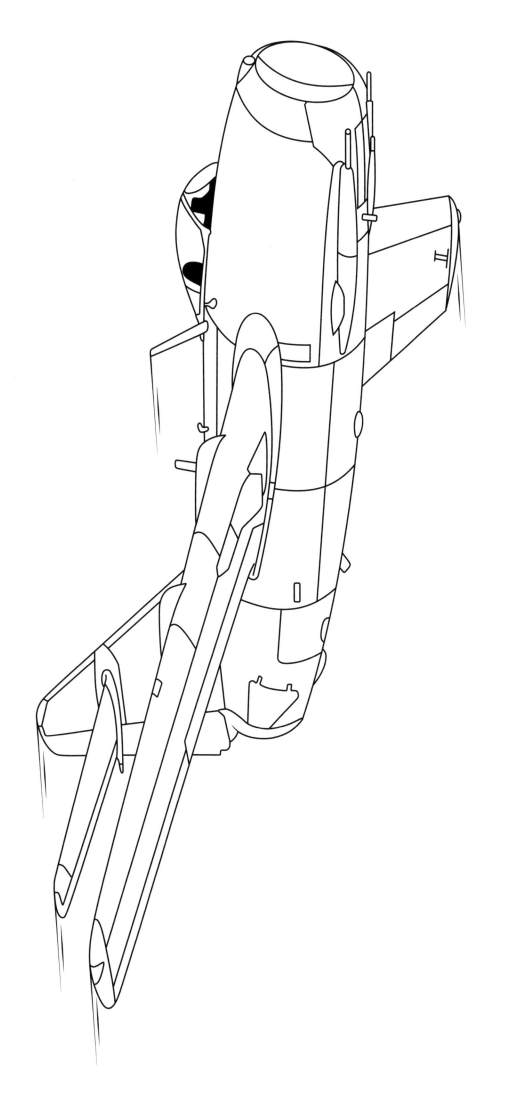

BOULTON PAUL DEFIANT

The Boulton Paul Defiant was a British interceptor aircraft that served with the Royal Air Force (RAF) during the Second World War. The Defiant was designed and built by Boulton Paul Aircraft as a "turret fighter", without any forward-firing guns. The lack of forward-firing armament proved to be a great weakness in daylight combat and its potential was only realized when it was converted to night fighting.

GENERAL CHARACTERISTICS

Crew: 2
Length: 35 ft 4 in (10.77 m)
Wingspan: 39 ft 4 in (11.99 m)
Height: 11 ft 4 in (3.46 m)
Empty weight: 6,078 lb (2,763 kg)
Max. takeoff weight: 8,600 lb (3,909 kg)
Powerplant: 1 × Rolls-Royce Merlin III liquid-cooled V12 engine, 1,030 hp (768 kW)

PERFORMANCE

Maximum speed: 304 mph (264 knots, 489 km/h) at 17,000 ft (5,180 m)
Cruise speed: 175 mph (152 knots, 282 km/h) at 15,000 ft (4,570 m)
Range: 465 mi (404 nmi, 749 km)
Service ceiling: 31,000 ft[35] (9,250 m)

ARMAMENT

Guns: 4 × 0.303 in (7.7 mm) Browning machine guns in hydraulically powered dorsal turret (600 rpg)

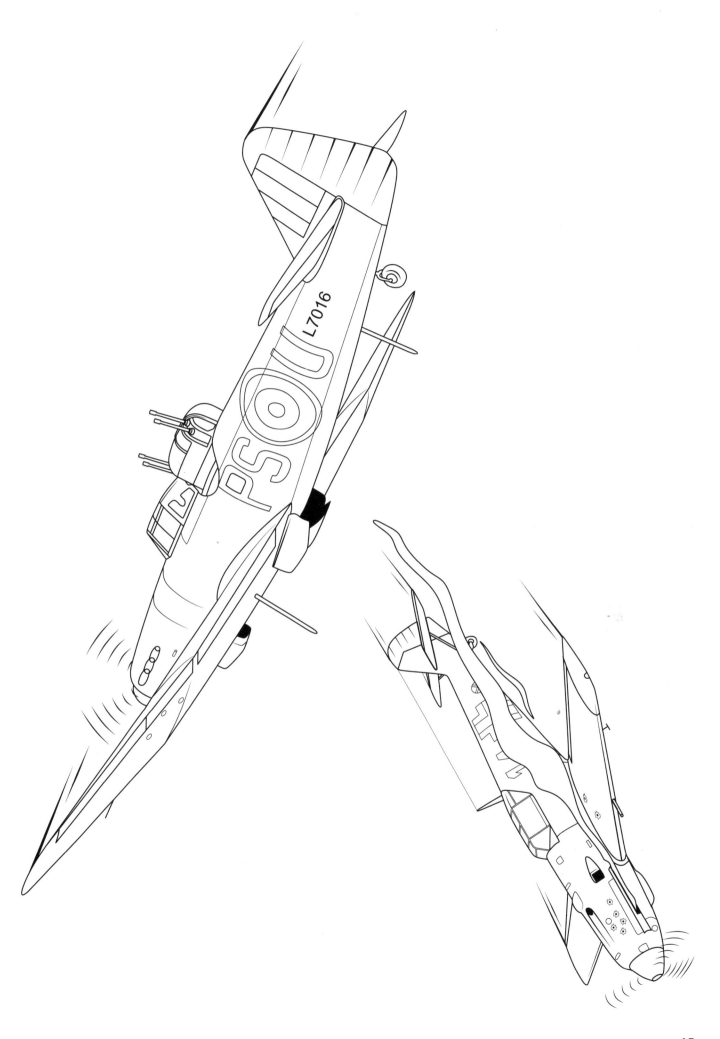

VOUGHT F4U CORSAIR

The Chance Vought F4U Corsair was an American fighter aircraft that saw service primarily in World War II and the Korean War. From the first prototype delivery to the U.S. Navy in 1940, to final delivery in 1953 to the French, 12,571 F4U Corsairs were manufactured by Vought in 16 separate models, in the longest production run of any piston-engined fighter in U.S. history (1942–53).

GENERAL CHARACTERISTICS

Crew:	1 pilot
Length:	33 ft 8 in (10.2 m)
Wingspan:	41 ft 0 in (12.5 m)
WS Folded:	17 ft 0.5 in (5.2 m)
Height:	14 ft 9 in (4.50 m)
Empty weight:	9,205 lb (4,174 kg)
Loaded weight:	12,405 lb (5,626 kg)
Powerplant:	1 × Pratt & Whitney R-2800-18W radial engine, 2,380 hp (1,775 kW)

PERFORMANCE

Maximum speed:	446 mph (717 km/h) at 26.200 ft (using emergency power)
Range:	1005 mi (1617 km) on internal fuel
Combat radius:	285 nmi (328 mi, 527 km) with one external 150gal tank
Service ceiling:	41,500ft (12,649 m)

ARMAMENT

Guns:	6 × 0.50 in (12.7 mm) M2 Browning machine guns, 400 rounds per gun or 4 × 0.79 in (20 mm) AN/M2 cannon
Rockets:	8 × 5 in (12.7 cm) high velocity air craft rockets and/or
Bombs:	4,000 pounds (1,800 kg)

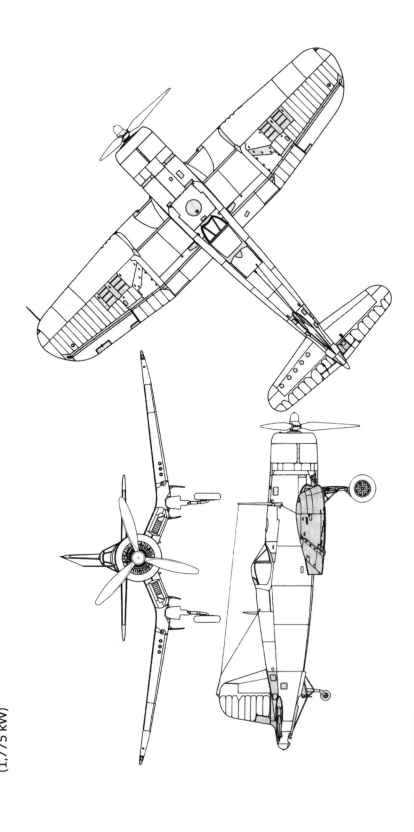

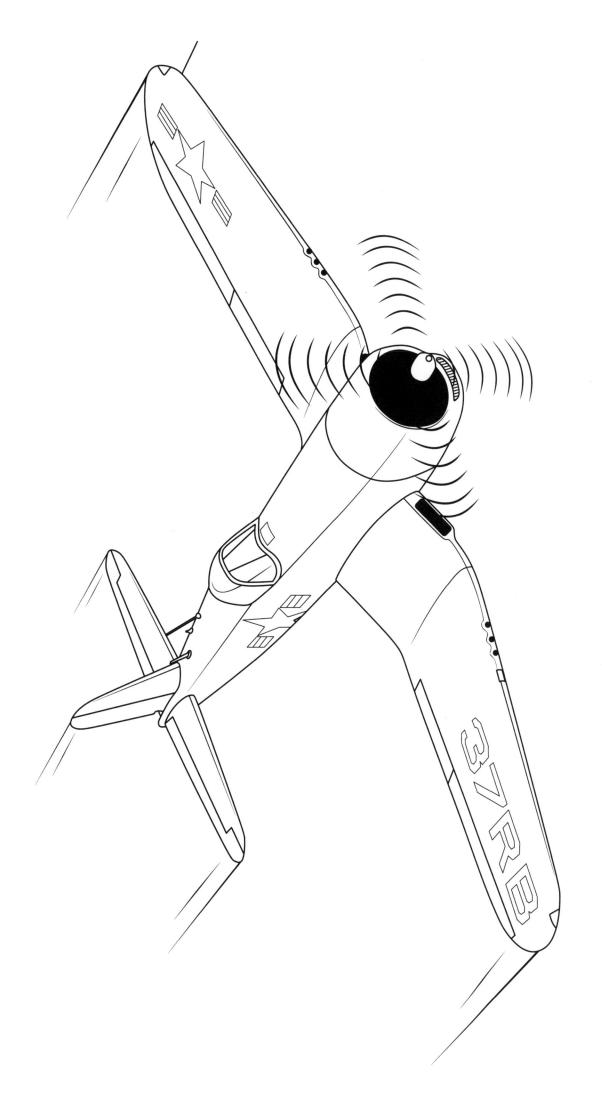

LAVOCHKIN LA-5

The Lavochkin La-5 was a Soviet fighter aircraft of World War II. It was a development and refinement of the LaGG-3 and was one of the Soviet Air Force's most capable types of warplane.

GENERAL CHARACTERISTICS

Crew:	1
Length:	8.67 m (28 ft 5.33 in)
Wingspan:	9.80 m (32 ft 1.75 in)
Height:	2.54 m (8 ft 4 in)
Wing area:	17.5 m² (188 ft²)
Empty weight:	2,605 kg (5,743 lb)
Loaded weight:	3,265 kg (7,198 lb)
Max. takeoff weight:	3,402 kg (7,500 lb)
Powerplant:	1 × Shvetsov ASh-82FN radial engine, 1,385 kW (1.850 hp)

PERFORMANCE

Maximum speed:	648 km/h (403 mph)
Range:	765 km (475 miles)
Service ceiling:	11,000 m (36,089 ft)

ARMAMENT

Guns:	2 × 20 mm ShVAK cannons, 200 rounds each
	2 × bombs up to 100 kg (220 lb) each

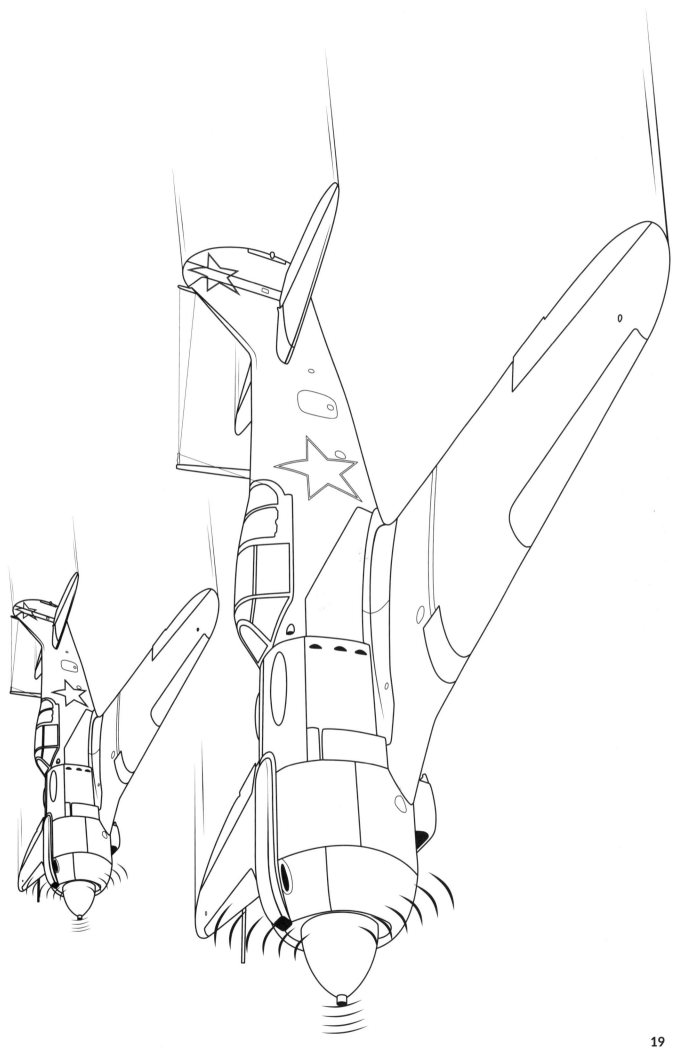

POLIKARPOV I-16

The Polikarpov I-16 was a Soviet fighter aircraft of revolutionary design; it was the world's first low-wing cantilever monoplane fighter with retractable landing gear. The I-16 was introduced in the mid-1930s and formed the backbone of the Soviet Air Force at the beginning of World War II.

GENERAL CHARACTERISTICS

Crew:	1
Length:	6.13 m (20 ft 1 in)
Wingspan:	9 m (29 ft 6 in)
Height:	3.25 m (10 ft 8 in)
Wing area:	14.5 m² (156.1 ft²)
Empty weight:	1,490 kg (3,285 lb)
Loaded weight:	1,941 kg (4,279 lb)
Max. takeoff weight:	2,095 kg (4,619 lb)
Powerplant:	1 × Shvetsov M-63 super charged air-cooled radial engine, 820 kW (1,100 hp)

PERFORMANCE

Maximum speed:	525 km/h (283 kn, 326 mph) at 3,000m (9,845 ft)
Range:	700 km (378 nmi, 435 mi (with drop tanks)
Service ceiling:	9,700 m (31,825 ft)
Rate of climb:	14.7 m/s (2,900 ft/min)

ARMAMENT

Guns:	2 × fixed forward-firing 7.62 mm (0.30 in) ShKAS machine guns in upper cowling
	2 × fixed forward-firing 20 mm (0.79 in) ShVAK cannons in the wings
	6 × unguided RS-82 rockets or up to 500 kg (1,102 lb) of bombs

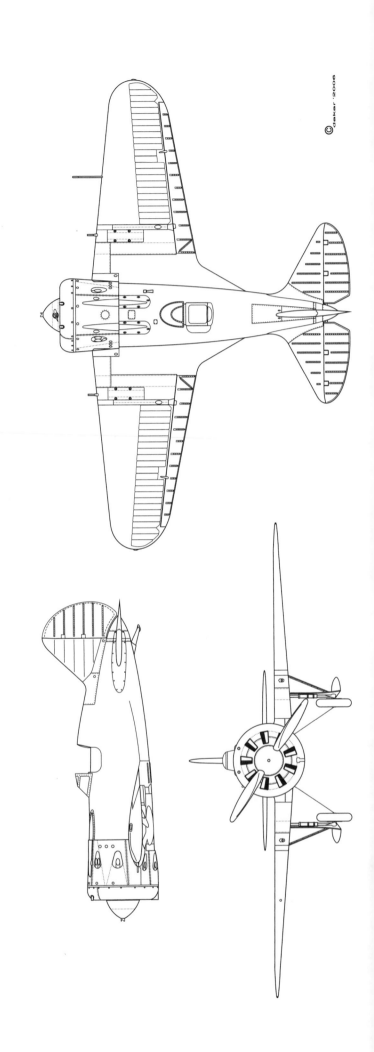

© daker 2006

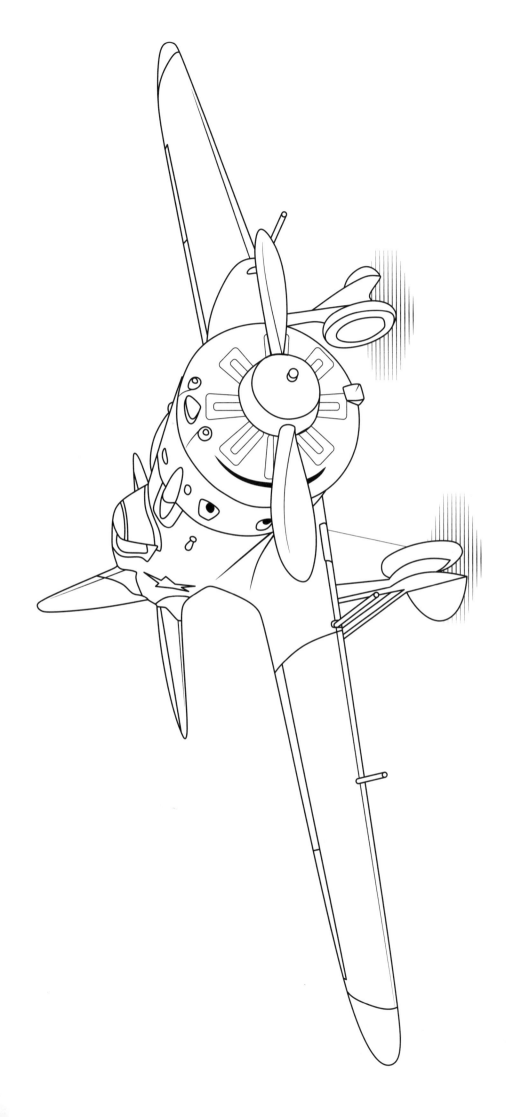

BELL P-39 AIRACOBRA

The Bell P-39 Airacobra was one of the principal American fighter aircraft in service when the United States entered World War II. The P-39 was used with great success by the Soviet Air Force, which scored the highest number of individual kills attributed to any U.S. fighter type.

GENERAL CHARACTERISTICS

Crew: 1
Length: 30 ft 2 in (9.2 m)
Wingspan: 34 ft 0 in (10.4 m)
Height: 12 ft 5 in (3.8 m)
Wing area: 213 sq ft (19.8 m²)
Empty weight: 6,516 lb (2,955 kg)
Max. takeoff weight: 8,400 lb (3,800 kg)
Powerplant: 1 × Allison V-1710-85
                    liquid-cooled V-12,
                    1,420 hp (1,059 kW)

PERFORMANCE

Maximum speed: 374 mph (602 km/h)
Range: 525 miles on internal fuel (840 km)
Service ceiling: 35,000 ft (10,700 m)

ARMAMENT

Guns: 1 × 37 mm M4 cannon in nose (firing thro
         ugh the propeller hub) with 30 rounds.
         2 × .50 cal (12.7 mm) synchronized Browning
         M2 machine guns, nose-mounted; 200 ro
         unds per gun
         2 × .50 cal (12.7 mm) Browning M2 machine
         guns (one each wing), 300 rounds per gun
Bombs: Up to 500 lb (230 kg) of bombs under wings
         and belly

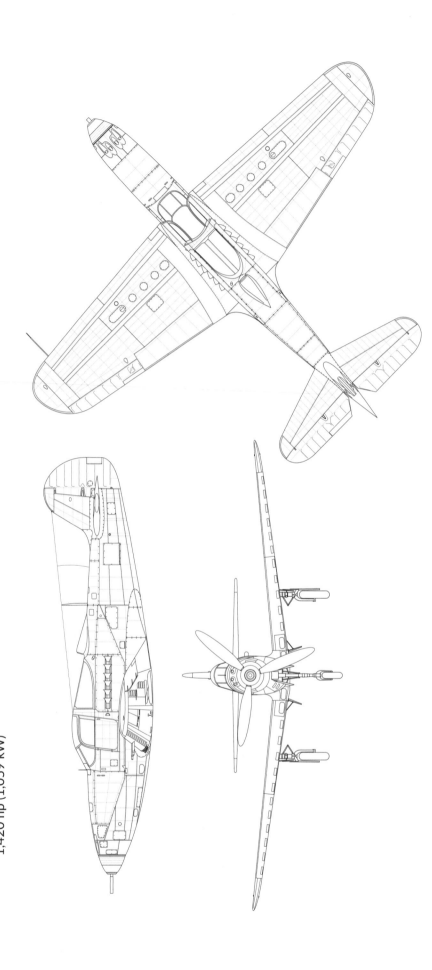

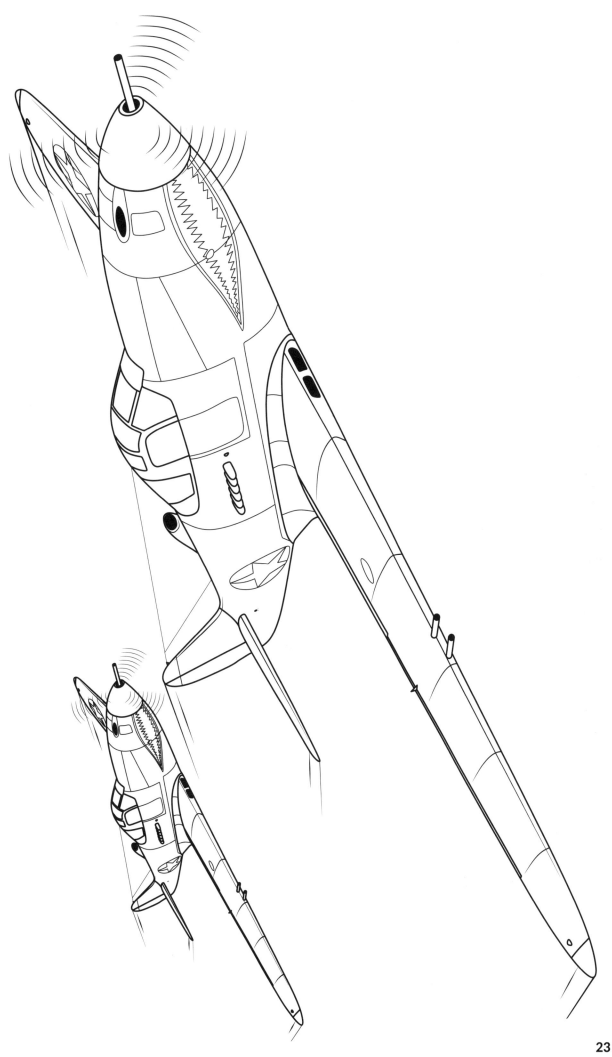

MESSERSCHMITT ME 262 SCHWALBE

The Messerschmitt Me 262 Schwalbe of Nazi Germany was the world's first operational jet-powered fighter aircraft. The Me 262 was used in a variety of roles, including light bomber, reconnaissance, and even experimental night fighter versions.

GENERAL CHARACTERISTICS

Crew: 1
Length: 10.60 m (34 ft 9 in)
Wingspan: 12.60 m (41 ft 6 in)
Height: 3.50 m (11 ft 6 in)
Wing area: 21.7 m² (234 ft²)
Empty weight: 3,795 kg[101] (8,366 lb)
Max. takeoff weight: 7,130 kg[101] (15,720 lb)
Powerplant: 2 × Junkers Jumo 004 B-1 turbojets, 8.8 kN (1,980 lbf) each

PERFORMANCE

Maximum speed: 900 km/h (559 mph)
Range: 1,050 km (652 mi)
Service ceiling: 11,450 m (37,565 ft)
Rate of climb: 1,200 m/min (At max weight of 7,130 kg) (3,900 ft/min)

ARMAMENT

Guns: 4 × 30 mm MK 108 cannon
Rockets: 24 × 55 mm (2.2 in) R4M rockets
Bombs: 2 × 250 kg (550 lb) bombs or 2 × 500 kg (1,100 lb) bombs (bomber variant)

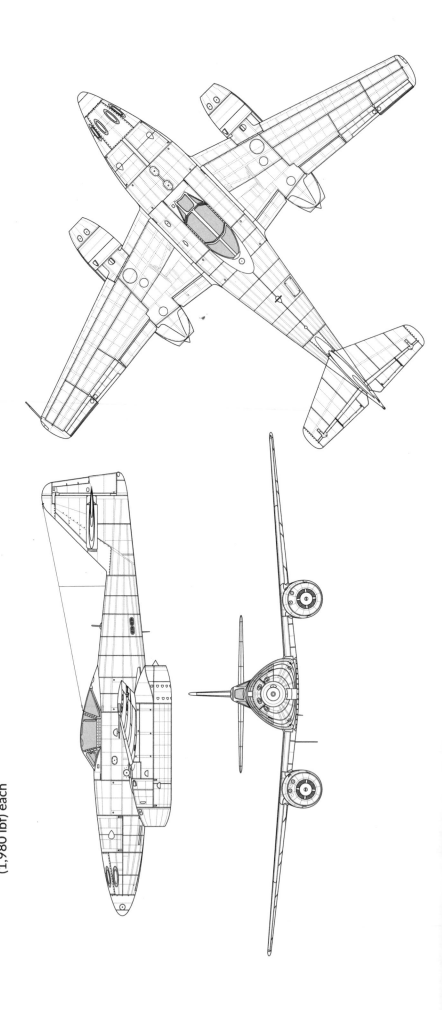

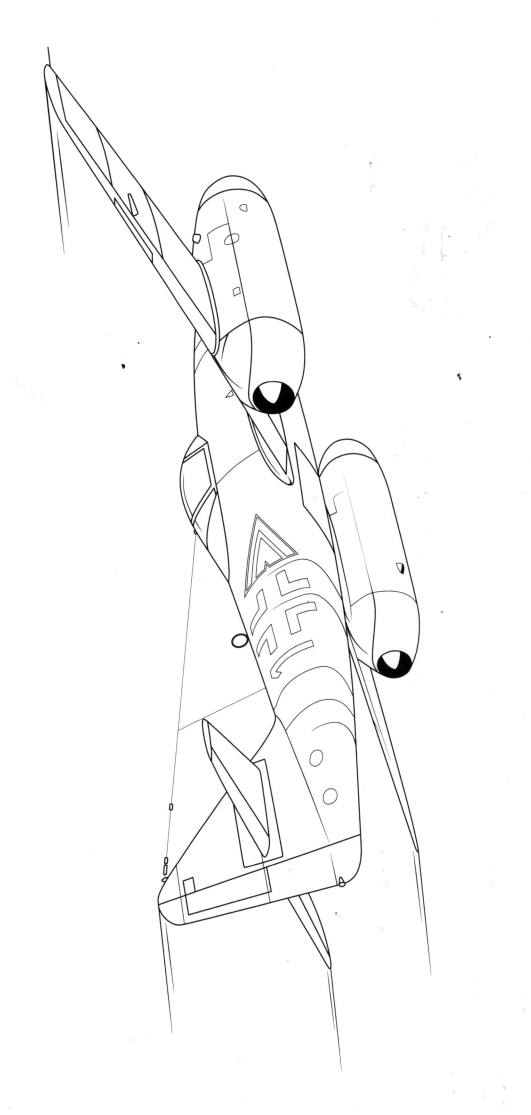

MESSERSCHMITT ME 163 KOMET

The Messerschmitt Me 163 Komet, designed by Alexander Lippisch, was a German rocket-powered fighter aircraft. It is the only rocket-powered fighter aircraft ever to have been operational. Its design was revolutionary, and had performance unrivaled at the time.

GENERAL CHARACTERISTICS

Crew:	1
Length:	5.98 m (19 ft 7 in)
Wingspan:	9.33 m (30 ft 7 in)
Height:	2.75 m (9 ft 0 in)
Wing area:	18.5 m² (200 ft²)
Empty weight:	1,905 kg (4,200 lb)
Max. takeoff weight:	4,310 kg (9,500 lb)
Powerplant:	1 × Walter HWK 109-509A-2 liquid-fuel rocket, 17 kN (3,800 lbf)

PERFORMANCE

Maximum speed:	959 km/h (596 mph)
Range:	40 km (25 mi)
Service ceiling:	12,100 m (39,700 ft)

ARMAMENT

Guns:	2 × 30 mm (1.18 in) Rheinmetall Borsig MK 108 cannons (60 rpg)

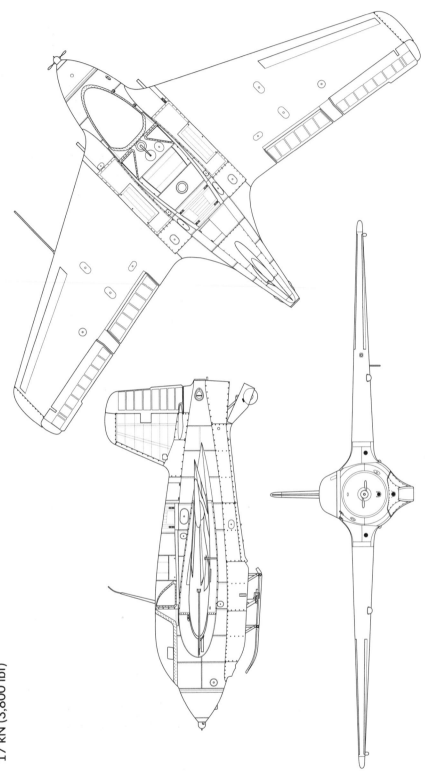

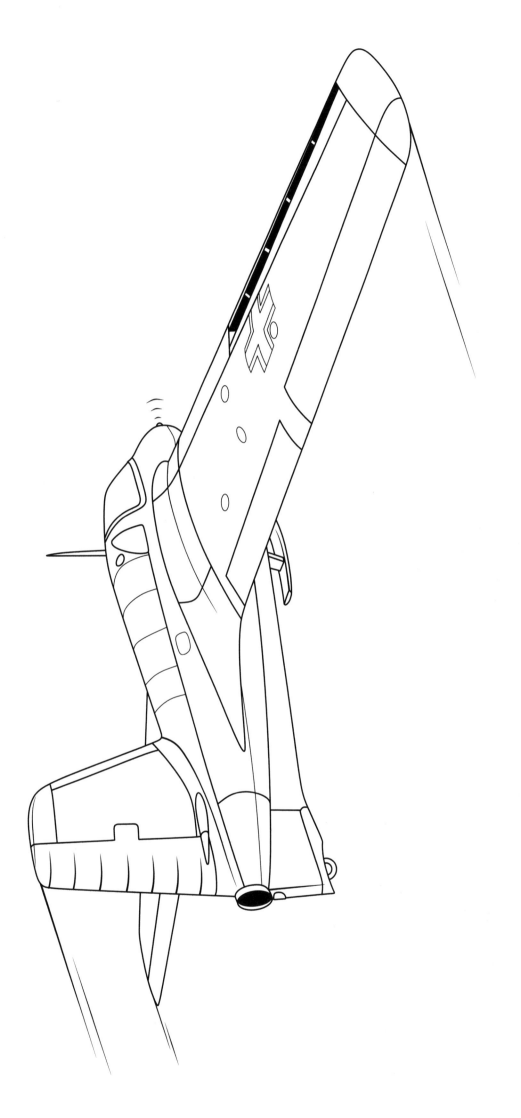

MITSUBISHI A6M "ZERO"

The Mitsubishi A6M "Zero" is a long-range fighter aircraft operated by the Imperial Japanese Navy from 1940 to 1945. When it was introduced early in World War II, the Zero was considered the most capable carrier-based fighter in the world, combining excellent maneuverability and very long range. The Zero was also adapted for use in kamikaze operations.

GENERAL CHARACTERISTICS

Crew: 1
Length: 9.06 m (29 ft 8 in)
Wingspan: 12.0 m (39 ft 4 in)
Height: 3.05 m (10 ft 0 in)
Wing area: 22.44 m² (241.5 ft²)
Empty weight: 1,680 kg (3,704 lb)
Loaded weight: 2,796 kg (6,164 lb)
Powerplant: 1 × Nakajima Sakae 12 radial engine, 709 kW (950 hp)

PERFORMANCE

Maximum speed: 534 km/h (287 kn, 332 mph) at 4,550 m (14,930 ft)
Range: 3,104 km (1,675 nmi, 1,929 mi)
Service ceiling: 10,000 m (32,810 ft)
Rate of climb: 15.7 m/s (3,100 ft/min)

ARMAMENT

Guns: 2× 7.7 mm (0.303 in) Type 97 aircraft machine guns in the engine cowling, with 500 rounds per gun.
2× 20 mm Type 99-1 cannon in the wings, with 60 rounds per gun.

Bombs: 2× 60 kg (132 lb) bombs or
1 × fixed 250 kg (551 lb) bomb for kamikaze attacks

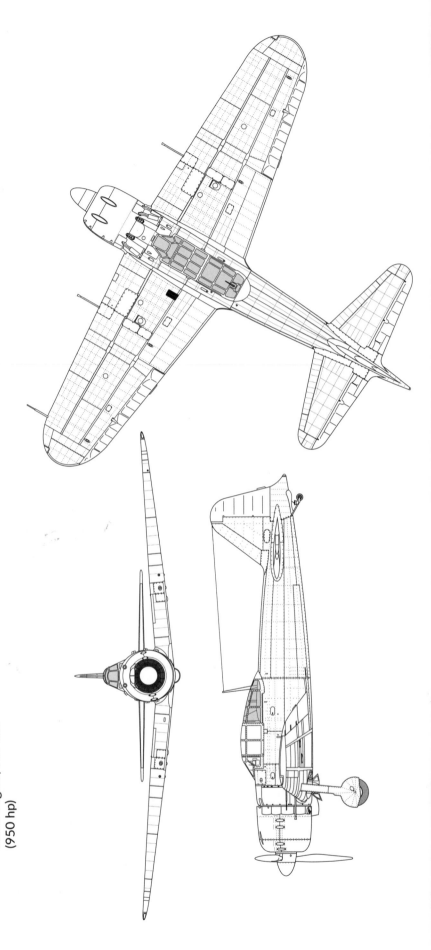

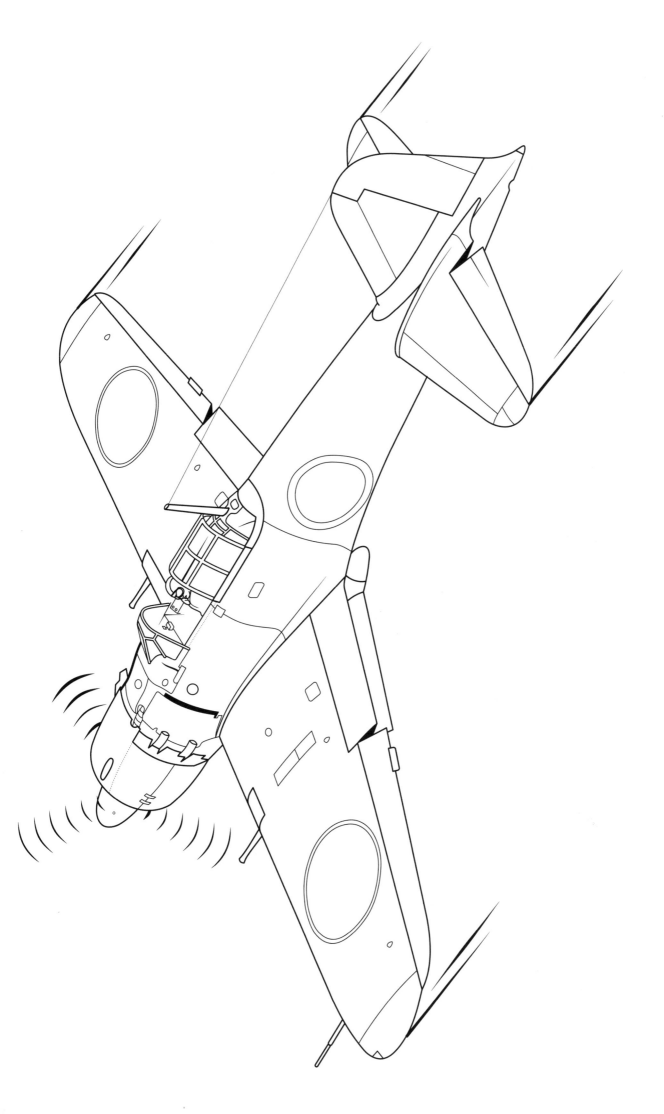

KAWASAKI KI-61 HIEN

The Kawasaki Ki-61 Hien s a Japanese World War II fighter aircraft used by the Imperial Japanese Army Air Force. It was the only mass-produced Japanese fighter of the war to use a liquid-cooled inline V engine.

GENERAL CHARACTERISTICS

Crew: 1
Length: 8.94 m (29 ft 4 in)
Wingspan: 12.00 m (39 ft 4 in)
Height: 3.70 m (12 ft 2 in)
Wing area: 20.00 m² (215.28 ft²)
Empty weight: 2,630 kg (5,800 lb)
Loaded weight: 3,470 kg (7,650 lb)
Powerplant: 1 × Kawasaki Ha-40
                 liquid-cooled   inverted
                 V12 engine,
                 864 kW (1,159 hp)

PERFORMANCE

Maximum speed: 580 km/h (360 mph)
Range: 580 km (360 mi)
Service ceiling: 11,600 m (38,100 ft)

ARMAMENT

Guns: 2× 20 mm Ho-5 cannon, 120 rpg each
         2× 12.7 mm (0.50 in) Ho-103 machine guns,
         250 rpg each
         2× 250 kg (551 lb) bombs

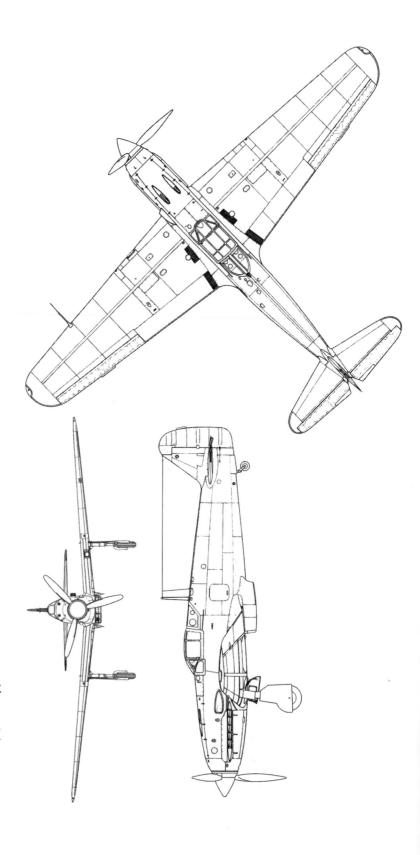

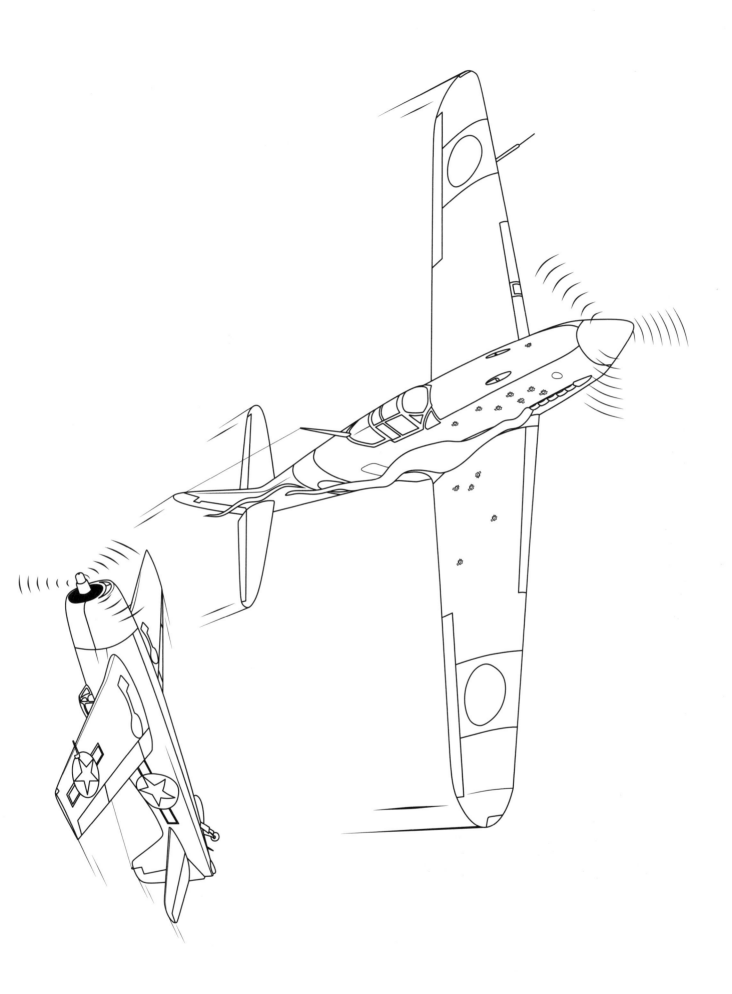

Published in Poland in 2016
by STRATUS s.c.
Po. Box 123,
27-600 Sandomierz 1, Poland
e-mail: office@mmpbooks.biz
for
Mushroom Model Publications,
3 Gloucester Close,
Petersfield
Hampshire GU32 3AX, UK.
e-mail: rogerw@mmpbooks.biz
© 2016 Mushroom Model
Publications.
http://www.mmpbooks.biz

ISBN
978-83-65281-19-7

Editor in chief
Roger Wallsgrove

Editorial Team
**Bartłomiej Belcarz
Artur Juszczak
James Kightly
Robert Pęczkowski**

Drawings
Dariusz Grzywacz

DTP
Stratus sp.j.

Printed by
**Drukarnia
Diecezjalna,
ul. Żeromskiego 4,
27-600 Sandomierz**
www.wds.pl
marketing@wds.pl
PRINTED IN POLAND